The Streets of
LIVERPOOL

© Colin Wilkinson 2012
Published by The Bluecoat Press, Liverpool
Printed in Slovenia by Latitude Press
Book design by March Design, Liverpool

ISBN 9781908457127

Acknowledgments
The author wishes to thank Francesca Aiken, the late Harry
Ainscough, Ron Davies, Getty Images, Barry Hale, Glynn Hewitson,
the late Karl Hughes, Liverpool Record Office, Alex Robertson and
Colin Weekes for permission to use their photographs in this book.
Also to the many followers of the Streets of Liverpool blog for their
support and many helpful comments.

Follow The Streets of Liverpool blog at
http://streetsofliverpool.co.uk

Browse www.fotolore.com for a fascinating and growing
archive of Liverpool photographs

The Streets of LIVERPOOL

VOLUME 2

Colin Wilkinson

THE BLUECOAT PRESS

CONTENTS

INTRODUCTION

In 2011, I published the first volume of *The Streets of Liverpool* in response to the popularity of my *Streets of Liverpool* blog. The idea behind the website was to encourage new thinking about the relationship between photography and Liverpool and to unlock hidden archives of images that rightly belong in the public domain. Happily, the book has been a great success and I have been encouraged to publish a second selection of photographs, along with my accompanying commentary.

The photographs of the changing face of Liverpool are a priceless resource, although their access is spread around numerous collections, private and public. From the earliest known landscapes taken in the 1850s, through to today's digital images, there is a treasure trove of memories frozen forever in time. We can look at Liverpool's waterfront in 1880 and compare it with photographs taken over the next 130 years and understand the massive changes that have taken place. We can also observe the harsh reality of urban deprivation and, in particular, child poverty, from the first hand-held camera photographs of the late 1880s, through to the stark images taken by photographers such as Thurston Hopkins in the second half of the twentieth century.

Photography gives an insight that no other medium can. One great benefit of the internet is that I constantly receive emails from readers who have added their recollections to photographs I have posted, from poignant memories of wartime bombing to more light-hearted reminiscences of days spent at the ice rink, cinema or seaside. I have discovered the names of the people in the photographs and about their life then and since. Streets and places, empty in the photographs, have become coloured with details and memories and transformed into a living history of our city. A patchwork of seemingly unrelated images slowly becomes one great people's history.

This book is a further selection from my blog. Over the last two years, I have posted over 250 blogs covering all aspects of Liverpool past and present. My commentaries are born out of the passion I have for this great city and the opinions expressed are hopefully relevant and interesting. If not, then just enjoy the photographs, most of which have not been published before.

On the Everton beat, c1963.

LIVERPOOL WATERFRONT

The top photograph shows Liverpool waterfront at the height of its economic prosperity. A radically different townscape from the one we are used to, although St Nicholas's Church and the dome of the Town Hall (on the right above the ferry) are two surviving buildings. Everything else has long since disappeared, from the warehousing lining the dock road, to the elegant colonnaded public baths designed by John Foster and opened in 1828. The baths served their purpose for the best part of 80 years before being demolished to make way for the filling in of George's Dock to create land for what we now call the Three Graces (the Royal Liver, Cunard and Port of Liverpool buildings). To the right of St Nicholas's is Tower Building, which was replaced by W Aubrey Thomas's white tile-clad building in 1908. Thomas, the architect of the Liver Building, created a building with crenellated turrets in an allusion to the original tower.

What is particularly noticeable about the photograph is the height line of the buildings. The scale is modest and in complete contrast to today's approach of building high.

SS Peruvian with the Church of St Nicholas on the left and, to its right, the spire of St George's in Derby Square. The dome of the Custom House is on the far right.

LIVERPOOL WATERFRONT

The top photograph taken in the early 1960s illustrates how the Liverpool waterfront had changed over 70 years. The change in the twentieth century was dramatic, starting with the filling in of George's Dock to create the modern Pierhead. In the 1960s photograph, the Cotton Exchange is still standing (its Edwardian baroque facade sadly demolished in 1967) but the Overhead Railway has been dismantled. Key 1960s buildings including the John Moores Centre on Old Hall Street have not been started and the White Star Building on James Street is still standing in isolation. An Empress liner is berthed at Princes Dock – in the final days before the liner trade switched to Southampton and elsewhere.

Fifty years on and today's waterfront is, again, dramatically different, with the new Museum of Liverpool, Liverpool One and all the other recent developments significantly changing both the landscape and the height line. Originally, the JM Centre was planned to have several extra storeys but had to restrict its height to be in keeping with its surroundings. Clearly the rule no longer applies, except in the thinking of the inspectors from UNESCO with their threats over withdrawing Liverpool's World Heritage Site status. Whatever the outcome, one thing is certain – in 50 years time, the waterfront will be significantly different from that of today.

11

SEAMEN'S ORPHANAGE, NEWSHAM PARK

Peter Ackroyd, the noted biographer, likened walking on London's pavements to walking on skin. I thought that was a clever way of capturing the human history of a city. Walking the streets of Liverpool, I can understand the pull of the past – even if Liverpool's history cannot match that of our capital city. My fascination with photographs is not simply with the changing shape of the urban landscape but with the people who made it come to life.

The photographs I have posted today are a good example of forgotten times and lives. The building is still there on Orphan Drive alongside Newsham Park, although derelict and waiting for a new use. Designed by that great Liverpool architect, Alfred Waterhouse, it was opened in 1874 to house some of the city's hundreds of orphaned children. By 1899, there were 321 children in the orphanage, whilst another 508 were receiving outdoor relief in the form of monetary grants and clothing. Children of all religious denominations were assisted, with preference given to orphans of British seamen connected with the Port of Liverpool.

I think the photographs of the three classes pre-date the Newsham Park building. In 1869, the Liverpool Seamen's Orphan Institution opened in temporary rented accommodation in Duke Street and, by the end of that year, there were 46 boys and 14 girls in residence. The success of the orphanage persuaded the Council to give land in Newsham Park for a purpose-built institution but the building in the background of the three photographs suggests the earlier temporary accommodation. The photographs were taken by Simon Kruger, who had a studio at 171 Park Road in 1871.

I bought the three photographs together, which suggests they belonged to one person. Perhaps in each photograph is a member of the same family: three siblings facing an uncertain future as orphans. I imagine they were treasured before being passed on to the next generation and then the next until their family name was finally lost.

Liverpool's cemeteries are fascinating places, where the famous lie next to the forgotten, and the infamous next to the virtuous. Anfield Cemetery is no exception. It will be 150 years old next year and its imposing gate piers on Priory Road are, in Quentin Hughes's words, 'a fitting announcement for the final journey'. Wander around and you

The Seamen's Orphanage photographed soon after it opened in 1874.

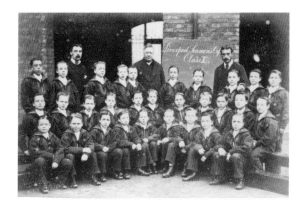

Classes at Liverpool Seamen's Orphan Institution's temporary rented accommodation in Duke Street, c1870.

will find the graves of Liverpool's legendary managers Bill Shankly and Joe Fagan, one of England's greatest barefist boxers; Jem Mace; James Maybrick, husband of Florence Maybrick, who was found guilty of his murder and served 15 years in gaol before release (he was more recently named as Jack the Ripper in suspect diaries found in Liverpool); and Bessie Braddock, the larger than life Labour firebrand. Look more closely at other gravestones and the names of those who never made the headlines predominate – which brings me to a fascinating email from Alex Robertson who wrote: 'Having seen the photo on your blog of the Seamen's Orphanage I thought you may be interested in the story of one of the inmates.'

Elizabeth Mitchell Ure (1882-1898) was the seventh child born to Thomas Ure and Mary Ure (née Robertson) on 28 July 1882. The family was living at 27 Woodbine Street, Liverpool when her father Thomas, a seaman, drowned off the Australian coast in May 1891. Her mother died a few months later in November, leaving Elizabeth an orphan at the age of nine. Thomas Ure junior, her eldest brother, the only sibling that was married, and his wife Margaret, took her in. She was attending Daisy Street School but, after two years with her brother and his wife, the situation must have changed because, in June 1893, Thomas applied to the Liverpool Seamen's Orphan Institution for Elizabeth to be admitted.

Thomas had to produce Elizabeth's birth certificate, their parents' marriage certificate, as well as a list of her brothers and sisters, together with their ages and giving reasons for her admission. He also had to give the name and owners of the ship from which their father drowned and he stated that his father, Thomas Ure senior, had sailed from the port of Liverpool for 35 years prior to his drowning. Elizabeth was examined by the orphanage medical officer and Thomas had to sign that she had been vaccinated against smallpox, had never had fits and was 'free from troublesome habits during the night'. The application was supported by Allen Bros and Co, who were shipowners and trustees of the orphanage.

After two months the application for admission was approved and, in August 1893, Elizabeth left her brother's family in Walton Breck Road and her old school for a new life at the orphanage. Elizabeth would have been given domestic training at the orphanage prior to being placed in domestic service on leaving. Tragically, however, she suffered two attacks of typhoid fever and died at the orphanage aged 15 on 15 May 1898. She was buried along with other children who died at the orphanage at Anfield cemetery in a double plot. There is a headstone with the names of all the children laid to rest there.

The impressive gate pier of Anfield Cemetery.

Elizabeth Ure's final resting place, along with many other children from the orphanage.

ST JAMES'S CEMETERY

I recently took a couple of American visitors around the Anglican Cathedral. Having marvelled at what I consider Liverpool's finest building, we then wandered around St James's Cemetery. It really is one of the most interesting places in the city and I am surprised at how poorly it is presented to the visitor. With the exception of Highgate in London and Necropolis in Glasgow, there can be few other cemeteries with such a dramatic setting. Sadly, the gravestones have been over-tidied up, but that only marginally spoils the impact. Every time I walk around it, I am reminded about the grim reality of Victorian life (and death). Only a handful reached three score years and ten, with an astonishing number dying before they reached one score. All around are the graves of sailors lost at sea in foreign places, soldiers dying in colonial wars, alongside the great and good of the city (including Kitty Wilkinson and William Huskisson).

Particularly poignant are the graves of the children from the orphan asylums, both boys and girls, with row after row of long-forgotten and little mourned names. Perhaps for many, it was a release from an almost inevitably desperate life of poverty and drudgery, but it is impossible to read the inscriptions without feeling deeply moved.

What is really needed is a cemetery trail – with information boards pointing out the graves of people of interest, as well as the history of the place. After all, Huskisson was the world's first casualty of the railway age, but his mausoleum does not give any clue. Nor is it evident how the horse-drawn hearses descended from the roadside down the narrow ramps cut into the precipitous rock face. We really do undersell the city – the cemetery is up there with all the other great (free) attractions.

16

The Huskisson mausoleum commemorates the first victim of the Railway Age.

The dramatic entrance to the cemetery through a steep tunnel cut into rock.

A poignant memorial to the children who died at the Female Orphanage in nearby Myrtle Street. The boys gravestone is next to it, along with one to the boys and girls of the Bluecoat Orphanage in School Lane.

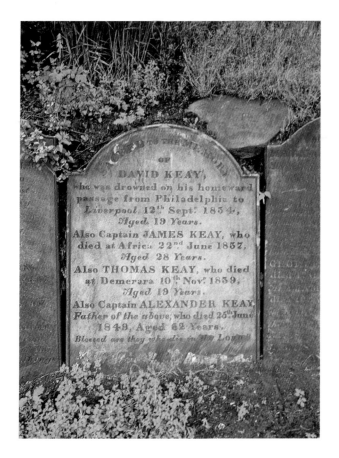

The gravestones emphasise Liverpool's ties with the sea and trade with the world. Among them is one to the unfortunate Keay family:

David drowned on his passage from Philadelphia in 1854, aged 19 years.

Captain James Keay died in Africa in 1857, aged 28 years.

Thomas Keay died in Demerara in 1859, aged 19 years

Their father, Captain Alexander Keay, died before them, in 1848, aged 62.

The sad story of Louisa Margaret Foy Wood, who died in March 1840, aged 11.

Her death was occasioned by her apparel having accidently taken fire. The brief period of extreme suffering which proceeded her dissolution, she endured with Christian fortitude and resignation.

MANCHESTER STREET, 1964

Manchester Street is hardly the grand street the region's second city deserves. Tucked alongside the Tunnel entrance, it is passed by thousands of motorists daily who probably give it only the most cursory glance. Before the tunnel was built, it had a more significant role, linking Victoria Street with Dale Street, but now, thanks to the Churchill Way flyover, it is just a dog-leg of a road cutting back on itself to Victoria Street.

The photograph, taken in about 1964, shows its short stretch full of shops, all long departed. The names will be well-known to many: Abraham Silver (tailors) next door to Eric's the Tailors, and Yates Wine Lodge rubs shoulders with Hessey's large store selling televisions in one part and musical instruments in the other.

Further down are, amongst others, the Catholic Truth Society Library, the Royal Tiger Club, Joseph Welsh (fish merchant) and D Samuels, another musical instrument dealer. The traffic policeman and the two traditional telephone boxes add a distinctly period feel to the scene, along with the pubs advertising Walker's and Higson's ales.

THE FLOATING LANDING STAGE

The Floating Landing Stage was a marvel of engineering. Originally constructed in 1874, it was consumed by fire before opening. Two years later, it had been rebuilt and, with additions, became the largest floating structure in the world, stretching for nearly half a mile. Sadly, in 1974, the structure was dismantled and replaced by a concrete pontoon, which sank, rather inevitably, in January 1976, only to be rebuilt. I suppose neither the old nor the new structures are of any great aesthetic appeal – purely functional – but the top photograph shows the original in use in the late 1880s.

Back in the early 1990s, I met a young American, Zane Branson, who was trying to raise funding to bring a Mississippi paddle steamer over to Liverpool as a tourist attraction. The timing was completely wrong and the idea went back across the Atlantic with him but, as the photo shows, paddle steamers were not a new phenomenon on the Mersey. The nineteenth century ferries were nearly all driven by paddles. What a great shame none has survived.

Paddle steamers at the Landing Stage, c1880.

The Floating Landing Stage photographed just after re-opening following the 1874 fire.

A liner at the Stage, c1900.

A liner disembarking, c1920.

The Landing Stage, c1900.

Enjoying a promenade, c1900.

FRANCIS FRITH AND LIVERPOOL

Early in 1912, John Sergeant fronted a BBC series on Francis Frith, the Victorian photographer who helped change the way we look at the world. I found the series deeply disappointing because it gave no real insight into the pioneer who spotted the commercial potential of taking and selling photographs of every town and village in Britain. This was a great shame, because Frith is so important to the history of photography and his photographic life started out in Liverpool.

Frith moved from Chesterfield to Liverpool as a young man and established a wholesale grocers at 85 Lord Street. In *Gore's 1851 Directory*, he is listed separately as a gentleman living at Beaumont Terrace, Seacombe. A founder member of Liverpool Amateur Photographic Association, Frith became enamoured with photography and sold his business at a substantial profit to pursue his hobby full-time. He made his name travelling to Egypt and the Middle East, where, under the most hostile conditions, he photographed the wonders of the Ancient World. His photographs were a sensation and, not one to rest on his laurels, Frith set about creating a photographic record of Britain that still survives largely intact to this day.

Many of his Liverpool photographs are of familiar subjects, particularly St George's Hall, which have limited appeal because they are places and buildings covered by many other companies. There were serious competitors such as Scottish firms James Valentine and Washington Wilson, as well as local Liverpool photographers. Their photographs were the postcards of the time and the popular attractions were the most saleable. Frith realised that the people sailing in and out of port were a good market and produced hundreds of images of the great liners associated with Liverpool.

The earliest photographic book on Liverpool I have come across was published by Philip, Son and Nephew in about 1875. The photographs are all by Frith's company and feature some of the great buildings in Liverpool including the Custom House, Exchange Flags and the old Adelphi Hotel. The photographs are hand-tipped in (this was before photo-mechanical printing was invented) and are rather lonely, uninhabited images (the exposures were so long that movement appears as a blur, so the photographer chose to avoid people in the photograph whenever possible).

Canning Graving Dock with the Custom House in the background, c1875.

Exchange Buildings and Exchange Flags, c1875.

George's Dock, 1875.

Church Street in the 1880s. St Peter's
Church is on the immediate right with
the tower of Russell's Building, a
victim of wartime bombing, beyond.
On the left is Compton House, now
Marks and Spencer.

LOST CHURCHES OF LIVERPOOL

One of the greatest losses to Liverpool's architectural heritage was its city centre churches. In 1899, both St George's Church (in Derby Square) and St John's Church in Old Haymarket were demolished (the latter being fairly universally disliked for its rather crude Gothic design). The elegant church of St Thomas, in Park Lane, was pulled down in 1905 (with the tomb of Joseph Williamson, the 'Mole of Edge Hill', left in the cleared churchyard). St Peter's was next in line, lasting until 1922. Its demise was planned for some time. In 1880, Liverpool gained its first bishop, Right Reverend Ryle, and St Peter's was made the Pro-Cathedral as an interim measure while decisions about a purpose-built cathedral could be made. In the photograph, the poster on the post states 'Full Cathedral Service'.

Once the decision to build on St James's Mount had been made, the diocese realised it could only fund the ambitious project by selling off its very valuable real estate in the city's main retail street. St Peter's had to go and there was no shortage of takers, including Harrods, who planned to build their only store outside London on the site. In the end, it was the ambitious American chain, Woolworths, who won and they maintained a high street presence for over half a century before Burtons/Topshop moved in.

I do find the removal of churches such as St Peter's sad. Not from a religious standpoint but because city centres need spaces that are not dominated by commerce and retailing. We have too few and need to seriously think about what kind of city we want to live in. Is all our space up for the highest bidder, as nearly always seems to be the case, or can we exert some control over its use for a greater communal benefit?

The loss of St George's Church was, perhaps, more serious from an architectural point of view, as the photograph opposite illustrates. An elegant church that stood mid-point between the Town Hall and the Custom House, it was demolished and the ugly statue of Queen Victoria erected in its place.

St Peter's Church, Church Street, c1880.

St George's Church, c1875.

MYRTLE STREET BAPTIST CHURCH

The church stood on the corner of Hope Street and Myrtle Street, on a corner site which is now a car park (facing the Philharmonic pub). A Nonconformist church, it had as its preacher Hugh Stowell Brown, who was so popular that the church had to be expanded to seat his growing congregation. The church itself was greatly admired although James Picton was a bit sniffy about its style of architecture: 'not up to the demands of the age in ecclesiastical structures.' Designed by WH Gee and opened in 1844, it did not see its centenary and was demolished just before the Second World War.

CATHOLIC APOSTOLIC CHURCH, CATHARINE STREET

The shell of this church was finally pulled down in the mid-1990s and replaced by a block of flats. It stood on the corner of Catharine Street and Canning Street and was a building that stood out from its brick built neighbours (what I presume was the presbytery still survives and looks somewhat out of place). Picton again was critical of the church's external dimensions but the church had a fine interior by all accounts.

ST MARGARET'S CHURCH, WEST DERBY ROAD

William and George Audsley have not been treated well in Liverpool. Amongst the most respected Victorian church architects, their two remaining Liverpool churches, Christ Church in Kensington and the Welsh Presbyterian Church in Princes Road, are in shocking condition. Possibly their finest work was St Margaret's on the corner of Belmont Road and West Derby Road, photographed in 1875 shortly after consecration in 1873. Pevsner considered it 'very powerful' and its interior was widely praised for its detailing and decoration. The church burned down in 1961 and was replaced by the present green roofed church.

The end of a fine church. The devasating fire at St Margaret's, 1961.

A MAGNIFICENT HERITAGE

What a shame so many of Liverpool's great churches have
disappeared, particularly since the 1970s. Fortunately, the city still has
some of the finest nineteenth century religious buildings in Britain;
the cast-iron St George's, Everton, and St Michael in the Hamlet;
George Edmund Street's St Margaret's, Princes Road; the Unitarian
Church, Ullet Road, All Hallows, Allerton, with its fine Burne-Jones
and William Morris stained glass; St Matthew's, Mossley Hill; Leonard
Stoke's St Clare's in Arundel Avenue and St Francis Xavier in
Salisbury Street are among the many of real quality worth visiting.

Three other very fine churches are illustrated here, or rather their
magnificent ceilings. St John the Baptist, West Derby Road, was
designed by the eminent architect George Frederick Bodley, in the
style of a decorated fourteenth century English chuch. St Agnes and
St Pancras in Ullet Road was considered by Nikolaus Pevsner to be
the most beautiful of Liverpool's Victorian churches, designed by
John Loughborough Pearson at the height of his career. The third
photograph is of the Synagogue, Princes Road, which was designed by
W & G Audsley, whose once magnificent Presbyterian Church of
Wales on the other side of Princes Road has been scandalously
allowed to fall into a ruinous state.

The Synagogue, Princes Road.

St John the Baptist, West Derby Road, Tuebrook.

St Agnes and St Pancras, Ullet Road.

39

SCHOOL LANE, 1970

I worked in the Bluecoat Chambers for over 15 years and loved the small group of buildings at the Hanover Street end that had survived against all the odds. Too small to be commercially viable, they were, nevertheless, a very visible reminder of an earlier Liverpool. Hornby Lowe's Cutlery Stores, with its superb frontage, was in business from at least 1879. The shop, with its macabre display of hunting, fishing and, I suppose, stabbing knives, was living on borrowed time, but it had a character that greatly added to the streetscape. Looking at my *1867 Gore's Directory*, the buildings had previously been occupied by an oyster dealer, a chandelier maker and a gas fitter. In 1857, Charles O'Donnell, a policeman, lived in the Hornby Lowe shop.

Once land values began to soar in the 1990s, their days were numbered. Few property developers have any respect for history; what are a few eighteenth century buildings when there is money to be made? The row of early houses and warehouses on Hanover Street was demolished one by one until the Liverpool One development swept away the last surviving building. Sadly, their demise followed the standard practice of removing buildings piecemeal, on the grounds that they are beyond repair, until there is no cohesion to the street, leaving the surviving building like a single tooth only too easy to extract. This sad pattern has removed whole layers of history: buildings not necessarily of great architectural merit but of importance because they were examples of Liverpool's first great wave of prosperity. Had someone suggested in the 1980s that the Shambles in York should be pulled down because they occupied valuable development land, there would have been a national outcry. The shame is that Liverpool lost so much with hardly a whimper.

THE BLUECOAT, 1966

The Bluecoat is the oldest art centre in Britain and has an illustrious history. During my time there, one thing that divided opinion was the Saturday art market held on the railings. How long it had been there, I don't know, but it was a free pitch for any artist willing to brave the elements.

You didn't have to like the art, much of it was too garish to my eye, but it brought a welcome dash of colour to the rather drab School Lane.

There were more than a few in the Bluecoat who wanted the Saturday gallery to disappear. It brought no money to the building and it probably upset artistic sensibilities. Whatever the reason, possibly the refurbishment which closed the building down for three years, or maybe the economic climate which made standing in the cold and wet rather unattractive if takings were low, the artists have gone.

I would love to see a determined effort to encourage them back. Liverpool city centre has changed almost beyond recognition; as a tourist destination in particular. Walking around, you are constantly aware of the different languages – French, Spanish, Italian, Polish etc – for, at last, Liverpool has broken through into the consciousness of mass tourism. There is a constant need to add to the visitor experience and this is one (free) way of promoting the city and giving artists a chance to earn a living.

LIVERPOOL AND FASCISM

A headline in the *Liverpool Echo* (January 2012) caught my eye. Liverpool City Council was considering having Wavertree's Cricketer's Club licence revoked after it hosted a conference of the British National Party. This brought to mind a photograph of a heavily bandaged Oswald Mosley after being attacked at a rally in Liverpool. Photographed at Walton Hospital in October 1937, he was at the end of his political career. A member of the aristocracy, he became a Conservative MP at the age of 21 but fell out over the use of Black and Tans in Ireland. Crossing the House, he became a member of the Independent Labour Party and Chancellor of the Duchy of Lancaster in Ramsay MacDonald's government before again falling out and establishing the British Union of Fascists in 1932. Heavily influenced by Mussolini, he quickly attracted influential support amongst both the Establishment and the working class. His more extreme supporters took to wearing black shirts and the *Daily Mail* published a famous headline 'Hurrah for the Black Shirts!' Rallies held by Mosley provoked violent scenes. The Liverpool rally was described in *The Glasgow Herald* newspaper:

Sir Oswald Mosley was hit on the head by a stone and knocked semi-conscious immediately he stood on the top of a loud-speaker van to address an open-air meeting at Queens Drive, Liverpool, yesterday. As the van was being driven to a piece of waste land, hundreds of missiles were thrown. Sir Oswald had not had time to utter a word when a large stone hit him on the temple and he fell on his face. Mounted police, who were standing by in a neighbouring yard, immediately rushed out and charged the crowd back. A Fascist bodyguard stood by to guard Sir Oswald, in spite of showers of bricks from large sections of the crowd.

Mosley was discharged after a week recovering from concussion and a minor head wound. Twelve men and two women were arrested, although whether they were Fascists or Anti-Fascists is not stated. From 1937, the appeal of the Black Shirts rapidly waned and Mosley was eventually detained in prison in 1940 for the duration of the War.

Liverpool has an honourable tradition in the fight against Fascism. Around 130 local men, including two City Councillors, fought in the International Brigade in the Spanish Civil War and 28 of them died in the unsuccessful battle against Franco. One noted participant was Jack Jones, later General Secretary of the Transport and General Workers' Union.

ON THIS SPOT IN 1720, NOTHING HAPPENED!

My doctor on Childwall Valley Road used to have a small brass plaque in the waiting room (a kind of tension reliever) which was engraved: 'On this spot in 1720, nothing happened'. I cannot remember the exact year but it doesn't make any difference. Searching through my photographs, this shot of nearby Score Lane struck me how apt that jokey plaque was. For centuries, Childwall was a quiet village on the fringe of Liverpool, popular with ramblers and day-trippers (particularly to the nearby Childwall Abbey pub opposite the church). Then, in the 1960s and 70s, this tranquil place was swallowed up by the city and the fields turned into housing estates.

I am fascinated by old maps, particularly those that show ownership of land. The map below (Bennison's Survey of 1835) reveals a feudal remnant still in the possession of one family – the Marquis of Salisbury. Do they still own land in Liverpool – or have they cashed in and moved on?

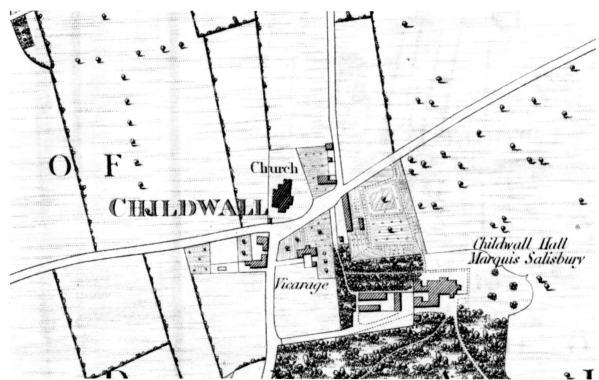

Bennison's Map of Liverpool (1835) shows Childwall as a country hamlet. Score Lane is on the left.

Score Lane c1900. The spire of All Saints church is in the distance.

LIVERPOOL AND THE BOOKER PRIZE

I drive down Booker Avenue every day, usually just after 9am to avoid the school run to popular Booker Avenue School. The road is a built-up 1930s estate, all neat and well-cared for houses, but there is a hint of antiquity for, in a railed-off corner plot lies the Archer Stone, which was a target for local archers according to legend. The photograph shows rural cottages being dismantled in preparation for new housing. Their existence points to an older history. Bennison's *Survey of Liverpool* (1835) gives a clue: just below the centre of the map is the land held by J Booker. According to the history of the Booker Company, the biggest wholesaler in the UK. In 1815, Josias Booker, the third of seven sons of a Lancashire miller, emigrated to Demerara to work in the sugar plantations. One of the first British settlers in Demerara, he learnt his trade quickly and became a planter of some distinction and, by 1818, he was managing his own plantation. Following his success he was joined by two of his brothers, George and Richard, and the firm of Booker Brothers was founded. After a dispute with the Liverpool ship owners who had been transporting their sugar, the brothers decided to form their own shipping company and, in 1835, they acquired their first ship, *Elizabeth*, a brig built in Scotland in 1832. In 1846, John McConnell went to Guyana to work as a clerk for the Booker Brothers, where he prospered and, in 1874, founded his own firm of John McConnell & Company. Due to his long and close association with the brothers, the two firms merged in 1900 and became known as Booker Brothers, McConnell & Co Ltd, and the company set up an office in the Albany, Old Hall Street, Liverpool, where it remained until 1941.

Booker became the sponsors of the prestigious Booker Prize for literature and three local authors have featured in its shortlist (Beryl Bainbridge, Linda Grant and Liverpool-born, JG Farrell, who won the Prize in 1973. Perhaps a less welcome link to such an important prize is the unsavoury fact that the Bookers' wealth depended on slave labour. Liverpool-born Farrell, who won with *The Siege of Krishnapur*, made a cutting reference in his acceptance speech to Booker's history of exploitation, which did not go down well with the sponsor.

Another connection, one of Liverpool's most famous comedians in the first half of the century – Billy Matchett, the Mirthquake – lived at 165 Booker Avenue from the 1930s until his death in 1974. Forgotten today, Matchett was mentioned by Ken Dodd as one of the two men who had most influenced him (the other was Arthur Askey). The Mirthquake (what a great name) claimed to have performed on every music hall stage in Britain.

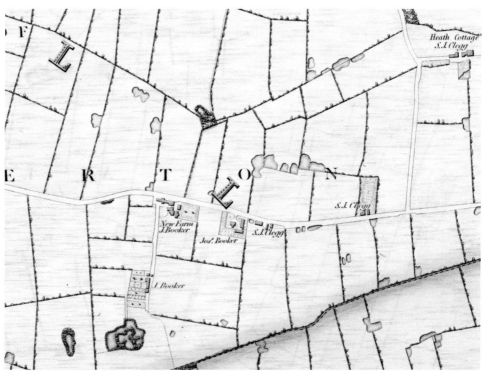

Bennison's map, showing Allerton's rural character in 1835.

LIVERPOOL'S CONCRETE GARDENS

I have always been somewhat bemused by the habit of naming Liverpool's inter-War tenement blocks 'Gardens'. A less appropriate word would be hard to find for those rather austere blocks. They do have their champions, amongst them architectural writer Owen Hatherley, whose recent book *A Guide to the New Ruins of Great Britain*, examines the legacy of the architecture and urban regeneration of New Labour. Travelling through Britain, he ends up in Liverpool where he compares the bungalow mentality of the Militant regime, to the 1930s schemes designed by Sir Lancelot Keay, Liverpool's City Architect and one of the leading planners in the country.

Hatherley complains that the great vision and confidence that took Hamburg, Vienna, Berlin and Rotterdam as its influences to create monumental architecture for the working classes had been reduced to uninspired suburban architecture that had been transplanted into key city centre sites. (Not just Militant – the last tenements were demolished as late as 2001 in Old Swan to make way for a Tesco store). The issues are never straightforward. Liverpool's rapidly declining population had precipitated a rethink on housing requirements and the tenements were no longer popular with tenants (indeed I remember filming deliberately burnt out flats in blocks off Park Road where tenants were hoping to be rehoused in the new houses that were being built). Grand architectural statements are one thing, the wishes of the public are another, although it is constantly disappointing why small scale public housing is usually so drab and uninspiring.

To quote Hatherley: *It leads to depressing juxtapositions – as at the point where the grand sweep of the major surviving thirties tenement block, St Andrew's Gardens, meets a piddling close of nineties semis, with the Metropolitan Cathedral in the background. The scale is preposterous, with the houses seeming to desperately want to be somewhere less dramatic.*

Fontenoy Garden, c1964.

Myrtle Gardens, c1963.

51

52

Gerard Gardens, 1966.

Photographs by Harry Ainsough

Gerard Gardens, 1967.

Photographs by Harry Ainsough

Tenements, Soho Street, 1967.

Caryl Gardens, 1968.

LIVERPOOL RESURGENT

If the term 'Garden' was totally inappropriate in relation to the tenements, what about the euphemistic use of 'Village'. Stockbridge Village must have been coined with more than a modicum of irony, but what about Central Village, the new development incorpoating the ex-Lewis's department store? My idea of a village is some distance from chain restaurants and a multi-screen cinema surrounding an artificial lake. No cricketers on the green, or ducks paddling under willow trees. Maybe a few Morris dancers might find there way there ...

I am actually pleased that the site is being developed. I just wish they had bought and redeveloped the shocking 1980s row of shops which replaced the original facade for Central Station (and almost led to the demolition of the Lyceum, that was saved thanks to the intervention of Michael Heseltine). One of the best features is the redevelopment of the Lewis's building. It was built out of the ashes of its predecesor, which was bombed in 1941. The post-War period was not a distinguished time for building. Materials were scarce and often poor quality and the rush was on to create a sense of normality. Constructed in 1947, Lewis's is a bold statement. Faced with Portland stone, it sits comfortably across the street from the Adelphi Hotel.

The *tour de force* is undoubtedly the bronze statue by Jacob Epstein, one of Britain's greatest sculptors. Known colloquially as 'Dickie Lewis' for obvious reasons, its actual title is Liverpool Resurgent – a proud figure striding forward on the prow of a ship. The three panels beneath, in *ciment fondu* are lively scenes of childhood, also the work of Epstein. Hopefully, when the redevelopment is finished, the sculpture will look even better set against the cleaned building.

RMS OCEANIC

April 2012 marked the centenary of the sinking of *SS Titanic*. The story of *SS Oceanic*, is a less dramatic one, although its fate was remarkably similar. Like *Titanic*, *Oceanic* was designed by Thomas Ismay, director of the White Star Line and built in Belfast by Harland and Wolff. Launched in January 1899, it became known as the 'Queen of the Seas', the largest liner in the world and the first to exceed *SS Great Eastern*. This dramatic photograph was taken of the ship in Canada Graving Dock in August 1899. *Oceanic* could hold 1,700 passengers and 350 crew and the photograph gives a good indication of her size when set against the small crowd in the dock.

Oceanic's short life had its moments of tragedy, including ramming and sinking the small Waterford Steamship Company *SS Kincora*, killing seven. In 1905, *Oceanic* was the first White Star Line ship to suffer a mutiny, which resulted in the conviction and imprisonment of 35 stokers, upset over working conditions.

Finally, in 1914, *Oceanic* was requisitioned by the Admiralty for war service and was equipped with guns. Steaming up to Scarpa Flow, it set out to patrol the seas around the Shetlands for enemy shipping. An accurate fix of their position was made on the night of 7 September by navigator Lieutenant David Blair RNR (previously assigned to, then reassigned from *Titanic*). While everyone on the bridge thought they were well to the southwest of the Isle of Foula, they were, in fact, an estimated 13 to 14 miles off course and on the wrong side of the island. This put them directly in the path of a reef, the notorious Shaalds of Foula, which posed a major threat to shipping, coming within a few feet of the surface, and in calm weather giving no warning sign whatsoever.

Captain Slayter had retired after his night watch, unaware of the situation, with orders to steer to Foula. Captain Smith took over the morning watch and, with his former knowledge of the ship, was only happy when the ship was in open sea. Having previously disagreed with his naval superior about dodging around the island, he instructed the navigator to plot a course out to sea. Slayter must have felt the course change, as he reappeared on the bridge to countermand Smith's order and made what turned out to be a hasty and ill-informed judgement which resulted in the ship running directly on to the Shaalds on the morning of 8 September. She was wrecked in calm and clear weather. She was the first Allied passenger ship to be lost in the war.

Both Captains were acquitted at court martial. Lieutenant Blair, who had survived *Titanic's* sinking, was not so lucky and was court martialed for fixing the wrong course.

Every now and then, I post a photograph that reveals a bit of Liverpool's less savoury history. On 7 May 1915, the Cunarder *RMS Lusitania* was sunk by a German U-boat off the tip of southern Ireland killing 1,198 of the 1,959 people aboard. The sinking was a key moment in the First World War, influencing the United States to abandon their neutrality. Controversy has raged over whether *Lusitania* was a legitimate war target because she was carrying weapons and munitions.

In Liverpool, the news of the *Lusitania's* sinking was met with a violent reaction. The *Liverpool Echo* reported rioting that broke out on 11 May: *A large pork shop at the corner of Smithdown Road and Arundel Avenue had been absolutely wrecked, all the windows had been smashed and the stock commandeered or thrown into the street. Women hurled strings of sausages at one another and one woman from a neighbouring street went down on her knees and scrubbed the pavement with a joint of pork. Other women went home with their aprons full of pork and bacon. After sacking the shops, the invaders went into the living room upstairs and spread destruction …*

In *The Autobiography of a Liverpool Slummy*, Pat O'Mara's account makes fascinating reading and captures the mood of both anger and opportunism that swept through the mob: *That night Freddie and I … started for a dance over Paddy's Market in St Martin's Hall. We never attended it, however. Before entering the Hall, we walked around Scotland Road listening to the cries of the women whose husbands had gone down with the 'Lusy' and we heard the bitter threats against Germany and anything with a German name. We walked down Bostock Street, where practically every blind was drawn in token of a death. All these little houses were occupied by Irish coal-trimmers and firemen and sailormen on the* Lusitania *… On the corner of Scotland Road, ominous gangs were gathering – men and women, very drunk and very angry. Something was afoot; we could sense that and, like good slummy boys, we crowded around, eager to help in any disturbance. Suddenly, something crashed up the road near Ben Jonson Street, followed in turn by another terrific crash of glass. We ran up the road. A pork butcher's had had its front window knocked in with a brick and a crowd of men and women were wrecking the place – everything suggestive of Germany was being smashed to pieces.*

Pat O'Mara headed back to home territory in Park Street to continue the 'fun', helping destroy Mr Cook's butcher's shop, for although Mr Cook was a patriotic Yorkshireman, his sin was to sell pork. (Pat O'Mara adds that he began to get sick from all the free sausage he had been eating). His account is a rare and excellent eyewitness account of a mob in action, written by the hand of an active participant.

The photograph of the Britannia Hotel at 283 Breck Road, on the corner with
Coniston Road shows how widespread the rioting was. Charles Claus Bobbie was
the licensee – Liverpool-born but of German parentage. I received an interesting
response from Charles Bobbie's great-granddaughter who wrote that her great-aunt
lived to the age of 103 and often mentioned the horror of that day and that, a short
time after, the couple's son was killed in France fighting for the British army.

CHILD POVERTY, 1910

Three barefoot boys sitting on a bridge spanning the Leeds-Liverpool Canal. I am not sure of the exact spot but I am sure some reader will know it.

This is Liverpool only a century ago. The photograph, taken by an unknown photographer, shows how tough life was for those at the bottom of the pile. This was 1910 and Liverpool was boasting to the world how important it was by building a cathedral and totally reshaping Pierhead. There was still plenty of money at the top but for all of these lads, life's struggle had already begun.

Boys enjoying a summer's day by the Mersey.

Not all is at it seems, however. A closer examination of the photographs shows the same barefoot boot-black sleeping in two different places. The photographer has presumably handed over a few coppers to get the right pose, possibly for his annual amateur photographic society competition. A popular category was street characters and these studies would have made a strong impact, one imagines.

Clearly, although staged, the content of the photographs is real enough. The boys were ragged, barefoot and living off their wits.

LIVERPOOL'S LOST PUBS

One of the subjects I get the most response about is public houses. It is probably a generation thing; to most of us over 40, pubs were central to entertainment and socialising. Nowadays, that is no longer the case and it is a sad fact of life that most neighbourhood pubs can no longer survive in a world of cheap supermarket booze, television and all the other attractions available.

It is hard to believe that so many pubs could have been economically viable until perhaps the 1980s. The breweries built lavishly and clearly expected a good return on their investment. There is still money to be made, as can be seen in the city centre and select suburban streets such as Lark Lane and Allerton Road, but for many of the rest, it is only a matter of time before the towel goes over the pumps for the last time. Here are some of the pubs that had time called some years ago ...

The impressive tiled remains of an Everton pub, 1973.

Gregson's Well, West Derby Road, 1973.

Trafalgar, Regents Road, 1975.

The Criterion, Brunswick Road, 1973.

The Soho Arms, on the corner of Soho Street and Richmond Row, 1976.

The Wellington, on the corner of Christian Street and Byrom Street, c1965.

Four pubs in one block on Brythen Street in 1963. On the right is the Old Royal, next door is Quinns, and, separated by a bird distributor, are The Dart and The Old Dive. All were demolished in the St John's Precinct development.

THE LION IN LIME STREET

It is reassuring to read that the Lion locomotive, one of the oldest in the world, is back on display in the new Liverpool Museum Great Port Gallery. The Lion was built in 1837, along with its twin, Tiger, to haul luggage trains between Liverpool and Manchester. In 1859, it was sold to the Mersey Docks and Harbour Company to be used as a stationery pumping engine. In 1928, Lion was presented to Liverpool Engineering Society, who renovated it and eventually passed ownership to Liverpool Museum in 1970.

In one of my first blogs, back in February 2010, I bemoaned the fact that statues of Ken Dodd and Bessie Braddock had been sited prominently in Lime Street station, yet there was nothing there to highlight its significance as the oldest mainline working station in the world. I have nothing against having statues of local personalities scattered around the city but these two are incongruous in their present setting. Likewise, I have no real objection to artefacts being housed in museums but, as the photograph illustrates, the most dramatic setting for the Lion is where it once stood until 1941 – on a plinth at Lime Street. Thousands of people pass through every day and the message made would be quite clear – you are standing in a place where the greatest transport revolution in history started. Museums are important but I believe that we can often gain more by the imaginative siting of such historical objects in a more dynamic context.

LIVERPOOL AND PICTURE POST

For many years, I have been fascinated by *Picture Post* magazine, which started in 1938 before the outbreak of War. Its innovative approach rapidly pushed its circulation to over one million. Many of the best photographers and journalists were recruited and it set a standard that is still remembered over 50 years since its demise.

I decided to research the magazine's coverage of Liverpool and managed to collect all the copies dealing with the city. Remarkably, apart from one feature about the dockers in 1941, nothing else appeared until 1949. Then, over the next seven years, a further eight features appeared, regrettably mainly negative in their concentration on urban poverty. This photograph by John Chillingworth was for an article 'The Best and Worst of Cities'. In the case of Liverpool, the emphasis was mainly on the worst. In my communications with John, who is still active in his 80s, he admitted to remembering little of his assignment, except for memories of a very tired string quartet in the Adelphi Hotel where he was staying.

THE NEWSPAPER-COVERED BED

During my research for my book, *Picture Post on Liverpool*, I made many unexpected discoveries. The most interesting story was of an article on Liverpool's slums, written by Fyfe Robertson in 1956 (who many older readers will remember for his dry humour and sharp television reporting). He was accompanied by his future son-in-law, photographer Thurston Hopkins.

I can find no trace of Robertson's journalism on Liverpool as the article was rather scandalously 'spiked' by the magazine's proprietor, Edward Hulton, after Liverpool councillors (presumably Jack Braddock and others) complained that the impending article was a slur on the city. So the feature never appeared, but the photographs survived (now in Getty Images' archive). And what a magnificent series they are! All unpublished, they give a shocking insight into the real poverty that was so evident in many neighbourhoods.

Remarkably, Thurston Hopkins is still going strong at 99 (He actually apologised for taking time in replying to my questions because he was so busy!). One photograph he particularly remembered was of a young girl in a bed covered with newspaper. The girl's grandmother had tipped him off. He was accused later of having staged the photograph but he said it was real enough. Every day, the girl's mother would cover the bed with newspaper to keep the rain from ruining the bedclothes.

How many others lived in such appalling conditions? No wonder the Council wanted the article buried.

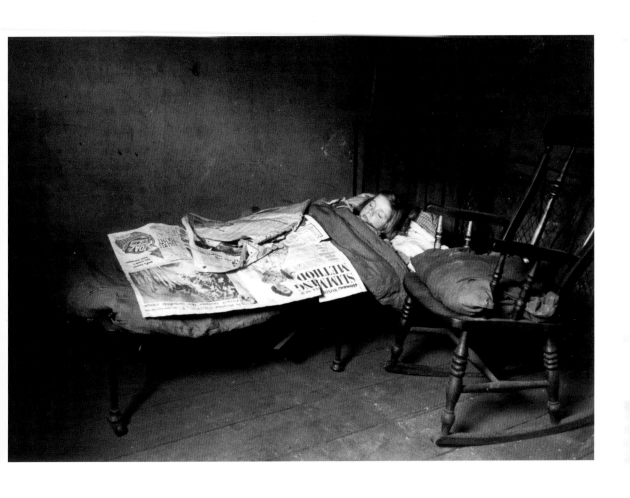

HOPE STREET, 1965

Hope Street is one of the few Liverpool streets that has improved considerably in the last 40 years. Buildings have been cleaned up, the new entrance to the Metropolitan Cathedral makes a dramatic ending to the streetscape, the Georgian buildings have found new uses and even newcomers, like the Hope Street Hotel, fit in seamlessly. Every September, the Hope Street Festival gets bigger, with dozens of food and craft stalls, live entertainment and open buildings, including the Masonic Hall. Along with all its other free festivals, Liverpool is reclaiming its crown as England's most exciting city.

Hope Street 1965. Construction of the Metroplitan Cathedral is well under way.

The London Carriage Works, 1973, now an hotel and restaurant.

The Everyman, before its first major refurbishment, 1973.
A new theatre is being built on the site and is due to open in 2013.

PHILHARMONIC HALL

A walk along Hope Street takes in a fascinating and eclectic mix of architecture. With two twentieth century cathedrals bookending the street, there is a solid core of Georgian and early Victorian terraces, the Art Nouveau splendour of the Philharmonic pub, the echoes of Rennie Mackintosh in the Convent of Notre Dame, the French chateau style of Blackburne House and the striking Art Deco Philharmonic Hall.

The original Philharmonic Hall, which was greatly admired for its accoustics, was destroyed by fire in 1933. Herbert J Rowse was appointed and, influenced by the Dutch architect Dudok, he designed a Classical building with a plain brick exterior, saving the lavish decoration for the interior. Rowse's other work in Liverpool includes Martins Bank and India Buildings on Water Street, George's Dock Building and the design of the Mersey Tunnel. Rowse was an architect who demanded the greatest attention to detail and used Liverpool's foremost artists and craftsmen to produce some of the best inter-war architecture in the country.

Some of the superb Art Deco motifs which enhance the Philharmonic's interior.

The original Philharmonic Hall, c1900.

Rowse's replacement – one of the finest concert halls in Britain.

NEAR TO REVOLUTION

Over 15 years ago, I published a book *Near to Revolution* by Eric Taplin, on the 1911 Transport Strike in Liverpool (not to be confused with the 1926 General Strike). In 2011, Liverpool City Council launched *City of Radicals 2011* to mark not just the centenary of the strike but a number of other events including the first Post-Impressionist exhibition outside of London at the Sandon Studios (now Bluecoat Art Centre), the death of Robert Tressell, author of *The Ragged Trousered Philanthropist*, and the first International Women's Day.

The strike itself should be seen against the background of a divided society, with 120,000 people owning two-thirds of the nation's wealth. The Industrial Revolution had widened the poverty gap, with millions living barely at subsistence level. Liverpool was a hotbed of activism and there was a growing feeling that a united labour force could take over the means of production. Inspired by radicals such as Tom Mann and Ben Tillett, 'war' was declared and industrial action began to spiral out of control. Troops and police from other forces were called in, *HMS Antrim* was moored in the Mersey and, inevitably, two strikers were shot dead in the most violent strike action ever seen in Britain. Winston Churchill, the Home Secretary, described the situation as 'near to revolution'. Panic resolutions to settle with the different unions began to take the sting out of the strike, which had lost some of its impetus due to police and military aggression coupled with the two deaths.

From a photographic point of interest, this was the first major strike to be fully documented photographically and cinematically (although only brief snatches of the film survive). Most of the photographic record is the work of the Carbonora company run by Gwilym Mills. His set of postcards published throughout the strike are now amongst the most collectible (reaching up to £100 plus per card). Unfortunately, the offices and workrooms of Carbonora were destroyed by enemy bombing and their negatives and archive destroyed, though the company still survives as the Mills Media Group.

The top photograph shows a police and army convoy travelling along County Road in Walton. The shops on the left belonged to Robert Crease, a music dealer, Arthur Rattenbury's tobacconist, and Elizabeth Ford's hosiery shop. The second photograph, showing troops protecting food supplies in Sefton Street, was an American Press print – which indicates the international importance of the strike.

An armoured convoy in County Road.

Troops protecting wagons in Sefton Street.

These two photographs are my favourites: the rather inadequate riot car (although petrol bombs had not been thought of at that time) and the boys playing cricket on St George's Plateau in the midst of all the mayhem.

After the 2011 riots in London, Manchester and Liverpool, amongst other places, I cannot resist taking another look back at the 1911 General Transport Strike. No doubt there will be some who can draw parallels between the recent riots in our major cities and the disturbances of a century ago. In most people's judgement, I imagine clear distinctions will be made between workers fighting for an improvement in their working conditions and the violence and mayhem of last year. There is one common factor, however, and that is the reaction of authority under pressure.

The threat of civil disorder spreading induced panic measures – the Riot Act was read out and handbills posted with the following warning: *Large numbers of persons have assembled in the disturbed streets for the purpose of seeing what is going on, and I warn all such persons that if the Authorities are called upon to act, innocent citizens are likely to be injured as those against whom any drastic measures on the part of the Police or the Military are directed.*

CANDID CAMERA

Since the 1990s, there has been a revolution in photography. The introduction of digital photography has given most of us the ability to record effortlessly and almost without cost, thousands of images that we can store on computers and post on the internet. A remarkable number of images is being created, although how so many photographs will be archived accessed and viewed presents a challenging problem.

Back in the 1890s, a similar revolution took place. Until then, photography had been largely limited to wealthy amateurs and professionals. Cameras were unwieldy and depended on tripods for stability. The glass plates used demanded relatively long exposure, since rapid movement created a blurred image, and also space at home to develop and print the results. Technology rapidly changed the status quo. Led by the American Kodak Company, portable cameras using celluloid roll film dispensed with the need for tripods and, more importantly, a personal darkroom. Kodak offered the first develop and print service – relatively expensive initially – that freed the photographer from the cost and worries of doing it themselves.

The result was a wave of enthusiasm that embraced an ever-widening part of society. Amateur photographic societies flourished, offering mutual support as well as competitions and regular exhibitions. The annual exhibition was always broken down into genres: still lifes, portraiture, nature etc. A popular category was street life and Liverpool could claim one of the greatest exponents in Charles Frederick Inston, a lithographic printer by trade. His work, and that of others, has created a fascinating record of Liverpool in the 1890s and early 1900s. Unfortunately, the images are not in a single archive but they exist in many collections, both public and private. Hopefully, with the advent of the digital revolution, many of them will become available in the relatively near future.

A ginger beer street seller in front of the old Tower Building, c1895.

A small bare-footed girl heads to the pub with an empty jug. One of a series of images taken by anti-drink campaigner, N Stephen, c1895.

Mann Island in the late 1890s. The steeple of St George's Church gives some indication of the date, as does the warehouse on the left, soon to be demolished for the headquarters of the White Star shipping line.

The irresistible combination of children and water made Steble Fountain a popular spot for the amateur photographer.

Street traders were one of the most popular subjects and the area around
St John's Market provided an almost unlimited supply of characters.

A queue outside the old Royal Court Theatre, c1900.

I know Liverpool tourism officials are always on the lookout for interesting news stories, yet the extraordinary claim that Martin Luther King's 'I have a dream' speech was written at the Adelphi Hotel is quite staggering.

A guide to an event entitled 'Liverpool Discovers', contains a map of more than 20 locations where famous people were born, along with places associated with celebrities and events in their lives. The guide proclaims: 'Martin Luther King visited his supporters in Liverpool three times, and the first draft of his famous "I have a dream" speech is alleged to have been written on Adelphi Hotel headed notepaper.'

After ridicule in the national press, the claim was hastily withdrawn. Apparently, the information came from a member of the public and was published without checking. So what about another piece of history. Did Hitler really come to Liverpool? Michael Unger, past editor of *The Liverpool Echo*, has just published his book based on Bridget Hitler's memoirs. Bridget was a 17-year-old Irish girl when she met Alois, Hitler's half-brother in Dublin. They eloped to Liverpool, where they rented 102 Upper Stanhope Street (in the photograph, the house is at the bottom right at the junction with Berkely Street. Upper Stanhope Street is the street joining up with Princes Avenue). Soon after, Bridget gave birth to a boy, William Patrick.

In November 1912, a dishevelled draft dodger arrived at Lime Street station. From then until April 1913, he idled his time away until, notified of his father's will being finalised (his father Alois had died in 1903), he returned to Austria much to Bridget and Alois's relief. Later, in the 1930s, William Patrick travelled to Germany to reacquaint himself with his uncle – who welcomed him half-heartedly. Eventually, after pressure to become a German national, William Patrick fled to New York with his mother and became a minor celebrity giving talks about Uncle Adolf.

So is Hitler's stay in Liverpool just another piece of mythology? Well, in the 1970s, a hand-typed document, the memoirs of Bridget Hitler, was discovered in a New York library. The question is why would a rather naive Irish woman claim Hitler had stayed with them in Liverpool? Her memoirs were never published and it would be a rather pointless claim to make if untrue. She was, after all, living in America at that time and had no reason to distort her life in England. The claim has been refuted by a number of historians – but they cannot account for Hitler's whereabouts at that time. Hitler was very careful to remove from the records most of the references to his younger years – certainly any suggestion he was a draft dodger. Back in 1913, he was just an ordinary German citizen, who could travel unhindered around Europe without records being kept – so I go along with Michael Unger.

LIVERPOOL AND THE BLITZ

It is now over 70 years since Liverpool was attacked in what is known as the May Blitz. The photograph opposite shows the physical effects of the bombing. Liverpool suffered more extensive damage (and loss of life) than any other British city outside of London. In terms of casualties, it actually registered the highest number of deaths per 100,000 population than any other city.

An email from Glynn Hewitson put the tragedy of the Blitz into perspective. Of course it was sad that many important (and less important) buildings were lost, but the loss of life and the heartbreak behind each death is the real story. Glynn sent me a photograph of his two-year-old sister Pat, scrubbing the backyard step, just months before she became a victim to the Blitz. Here is Glynn's story:

I was born on the 29 August 1939, a few days before the start of the War. I was kept in Liverpool with my sister, Pat. My ten-year-old brother, Frank, was evacuated to a farm in Hereford but ran away a few times and turned up back in Liverpool. My mother had to take him back and I went with her. The transport was only once a week and I remember we missed the bus in Wales once and had to stay on the farm till the next week. My father, Gerry, was a docker, in a reserved occupation through the war.

We lived in about five different houses through the war from Chambers Street, Everton, to Waterloo and Bootle, where we were bombed out twice. My sister Pat was killed there. With me only being a baby, my mother didn't like to talk about it, even when I grew up. The trauma of it all got to her very deeply. We moved to Wye Street at the end of the war and stayed there until 1971 when the old houses came down and we were rehoused.

Looking down South Castle Street to the Custom House, undoubtedly
the most important building lost during the War.

PITT STREET AND THE WAR

When I started my blog, my intention was to establish it as a forum for understanding how photography has recorded the city since 1850. I welcome contributions that further this aim and the information and photographs come courtesy of Francesca Aiken, Assistant Exhibition Curator for Global City at the Museum of Liverpool.

The first photograph, by Father D'Andria, captures the innocence of children playing in the doorway of Low Chung's grocery at the heart of what was then Chinatown. The second photograph is of Kwong Shang Lung's grocery on the opposite side of the road after a direct hit.

Just over seventy years ago, a devastating aerial bombardment struck Liverpool, ending lives, demolishing homes and displacing whole communities. It is in tribute to 'the spirit of an unconquered people' that Liverpool's Anglo-Chinese community were part of the effort to keep calm and carry on, piecing back together not just buildings but homes and livelihoods.

Pitt Street before the war, shaped by tall converted warehouse buildings and cobbled streets, stretched out under the constant watch of St Michael's Church spire, busy with dozens of Chinese businesses, from boarding houses to grocers and tobacconists. This was the birthplace of Liverpool's Chinese community, the destination for seamen from all over the world including Spain, the Philippines, Italy, the West Indies and Scandinavia – to name just a few. To the people who lived and grew up there, this was 'world's end'. Pitt Street was the place to go, bustling with shops and cafes all within easy reach of the docks. Kwong Shang Lung was one of the city's earliest grocers to specialise in Chinese food, trading from 1915 until the bombs fell in 1941.

CHINATOWN

During the Second World War the local population swelled to take on thousands of seamen working for Britain's war effort, including up to 20,000 Chinese seafarers – risking their lives on Merchant Navy convoys. Pitt Street became a comfort zone for thousands of transient seamen to while away their two weeks of shore leave.

Elsie Kuloi was just six years old when Edward Chambré Hardman stopped to photograph her as she perched on an anonymous Pitt Street step. The family lived on Dickinson Street, and when the war came, their top floor flat was less than desirable when the sirens sounded. Elsie and sister Lan, then in their teens, were not evacuated but would go with their parents to stay at a neighbours on the ground floor. Out of curiosity, Lan stayed behind, only to witness St Michael's Church take a direct hit from an incendiary bomb. She watched it fall, streaking down to earth and was terrified by what she saw. Hundreds were killed in Pitt Street and Cleveland Square alone, including 30 people at 14 Pitt Street, next door to where Kwong Shang Lung served his customers.

At the end of Pitt Street was a large open area called Cleveland Square where the RAF would inflate an enormous barrage balloon to ward off dive bombers and force enemy aircraft to fly higher into anti-aircraft fire. By 1940 there were 1,400 similar balloons across the UK and the spectacle of watching it being lifted above its tether of thick metal cable was something the whole street came out to see. Barrage balloons however could not prevent bombs falling from higher up in the sky and, in May 1941, Cleveland Square and Pitt Street were levelled to the ground.

Merseyside was stunned by the loss of life and the enormous fissures of wasteland now riddling the city centre. Similar to St Luke's, the famous "bombed out church" just round the corner, the spire of St Michael's survived a direct hit on the surrounding buildings and, what took German bombers minutes to destroy, took the City Council days to pull down completely. To many this was an even greater tragedy for the community. Built in 1816, St Michael's was a part of local life and dominated the Pitt Street skyline. Today, the congregation survives, meeting regularly at St Michael in the City, on the spot where Pitt Street once thrived. The whole area is now given over to quiet residential streets, semis and bungalows. Instead of dispersal, the old Anglo-Chinese community shifted, making Nelson Street their new centre with its Chinese Imperial Arch, the largest outside mainland China.

Looking up Pitt Street with the steeple of St Michael's Church in the distance.

THE LEGACY OF PETER ELLIS

Peter Ellis is a great enigma. Little is known about him but he is regarded as one of the great architects of the modern movement. His Oriel Chambers is accredited as being the blueprint for the skyscraper. Built in 1864, it outraged architectural critics at the time, who compared it to a greenhouse. Ellis's radical rejection of traditional styles and materials was an attempt to resolve the problem of lighting in offices. The prevailing Gothic style allowed for fairly meagre windows, which resulted in dark and oppressive interiors. Even as late as 1931, Professor Charles Reilly was deriding the building as 'a cellular habitation for the human insect', although he hoped that it would survive as a humorous asset to Liverpool.

American architects took a different view. Quentin Hughes in *Liverpool: City of Architecture* describes it as the 'most significant office building in Liverpool and one of the most important buildings in the world, because, stylistically and structurally, it foreshadows, by many years, the work of the Modern Movement in architecture.'

Number 16 Cook Street is a lesser building but no less interesting in its expansive use of glass and, particularly, the magnificent glazed cast-iron staircase in its courtyard, an idea successfully exported to Chicago and used in early skyscrapers.

I started to research Ellis because no other work by him is known to survive. It is said he was so hurt by the criticism of his two buildings that he never designed another and continued with his other job as a surveyor. I am not convinced the story ends there. I have discovered that a Peter Ellis of Liverpool had applied for patents for lift designs at about the same time. Perhaps he found a more elevated career with ever-upward prospects!

The stunning glass facade of Oriel Chambers, one of the most important nineteenth century buildings in Britain.

The cast-iron staircase at 16 Cook Street is another example of Ellis's radical design that influenced skyscraper building in America.

One of the great pleasures of walking through the city centre is to look above the ground floor, where too often the ubiquitous branding by national companies takes away all individuality. Look above their fascias and the detail is fascinating, from Classical to Gothic, from parapets to domes. Here are two fine examples, of Castle Street and Victoria Street.

The green-turreted building in the top right photograph is the Adelphi Bank building. At street level, its imposing bronze doors are a reminder of Liverpool's great banking history.

Castle Street.

Victoria Street.

LAWRENCE ROAD, c1910

The 'Golden Age' of postcards, at the turn of the twentieth century was a time when commercial photographers would trawl the streets for customers who would pay for small runs of real photographic postcards of their business, home and family. This view of Lawrence Road is one such postcard, which could be sold to any one of the shops shown. The campanile of St Bridget's Church is to the left (a very interesting interior if you can get access – one of the city's hidden gems) and the baker's shop of Walter Moore can be seen on the corner of Portman Road. The shops in view are a typical good mix of the times. On the far corner is James Hanson (dairy), a sub-post office, John Hughes (grocer), William Johnson (fishmonger), Daniel Higgin (butcher) and William Hargreaves (greengrocer). Just one small stretch of the road and all the basics provided for. It must have been a profitable area because Hargreaves had another shop two blocks further on, at the corner of Bagot Street. Lawrence Road was a thriving street, in spite of being relatively close to the city centre. Other shops included a drapers, bookseller, tobacconist, shoe and boot dealer, stationers and chandlers.

How different from today with the almost unstoppable spread of the supermarket. I cannot imagine there is much money in selling postcards of nearby Asda, Tesco or Aldi.

LARK LANE, 1893

Here is a previously unpublished photograph of Lark Lane in 1893. The horse-drawn omnibus is advertising the Liverpool Overhead Railway, which had commenced services in January of that year. The shops behind the omnibus are William Truesdale (grocer), Elizabeth Handley (tobacconist) and, on the right of Truesdale, Arnold Thomas (glass and china dealer) and the Wesleyan Chapel.

Back then, Lark Lane had a good mix of shops, including bakers, shoe and boot manufacturers, a stationer, a saddler, milliner, fish and game dealer, grocers, butcher etc.

Sadly, like many similar suburban shopping streets, the diversity has gone; in Lark Lane's case to be replaced mostly by bars and restaurants. Perhaps with the ever-increasing cost of transport, people will look towards local areas more favourably, although the relentless spread of supermarkets has probably seen off all but a few specialists. How many more supermarkets does South Liverpool need? Should we care? I think the list of trades in 1893, and the skills they represented, says we should. Why can't we turn back the clock and recreate suburban centres of specialist retailers who care about serving their community.

103

ODEON, LONDON ROAD, 1954

When this photograph of the Odeon, London Road, was taken, the cinema was just 20 years old. The cinema was built on the site of a boxing stadium which had closed in 1931 and opened as the Paramount in 1934. Its opening was not without incident as the Scala, Futurist and Palais de Luxe all objected to it on the grounds that the Paramount company produced, distributed and exhibited films – making competition virtually impossible. The objections were overruled and a state of the art cinema erected. Interestingly, the frontage was restricted to about half the building's width because of the presence of the neighbouring store. The architect made up for the lack of width by building tall, with a distinctive stonework central feature which was illuminated by neon lights.

The cinema was designed for a single screen with stalls and a circle and a seating capacity of 2,670 (1,972 in the stalls and 698 in the circle). A resident organist gave shows every day and was in almost continual employment until the cinema was split into twin screens in 1968. In 1942, Paramount sold the cinema to the Odeon Deutsch group and it was renamed the Odeon. In 1954, the year of the photograph, it became the first Merseyside cinema to be equipped for CinemaScope films, later replaced by the larger ToddAO system (the screen was 51 x 24.5 feet). Following a record run of *The Sound of Music*, the cinema converted to twin screens. All the architectural features in the foyer and auditorium were lost in the conversion, which introduced Panavision and full stereo sound. One particular point of interest was the performances of The Beatles at the cinema in the early 1960s (before conversion). In 1973, an additional screen was added, followed in quick succession by a fourth and fifth screen (in 1979), followed by further subdivisions which finally gave the cinema ten screens by 1999. This was to mark the end of development, and the opening of Odeon's new cinema in Liverpool One was to prove the end of the road for a cinema that had provided great entertainment for over 60 years. The Odeon has now been demolished and a temporary car park now fills its space.

The Odeon in 1954.

The Odeon shortly after a fourth and fifth screen had been added in 1979.

LANDER ROAD SCHOOL

Lander Road is a short road between Linacre Lane and Webster Street, not an area I am well-acquainted with. I was about to make the ill-judged remark that the school had probably long-gone but a check on Google satellite revealed that it is still there. I have commented before that an illustrated book on Liverpool schools would make an important addition to the bookshelves of those interested in local history – after all, we have all been through the system and most of us have happy memories, particularly of junior school.

What is noticeable is that the children are dressed in their best and a look at my *1910 Gore's Directory* reveals a solid aspiring working-class area with joiners, plumbers, mariners, tram guards, carters, tanners and dock gatesmen among the trades represented on Lander Road.

Further valuable information came from Allan Johnson, ex-Deputy Head of Beach Road School: *The gentleman top left is, I believe, Walter Tomkins (also in the second photo). By 1903, Lander Road soon became over-subscribed and had to expand into temporary premises in nearby Scarisbrick Avenue. In 1905, there were 347 children and five teachers and Tomkins moved across to become the Head. When new schools opened in Beach Road in 1908, he became Head of the Boys School, remaining there until his death in May 1941 (killed outside his home when bombs fell nearby). He was a very well respected member of the local community. The gentleman with Tomkins in the two photos is, I think, Mr Lowe. He was head of Lander Road and, on Tomkins' death, took over at Beach Road. Both men have memorial plaques in the – now empty – former Beach Road premises. The plaque to Tomkins, erected by staff and parents after his death, was meant to go to Litherland British Legion Club on the closure of Beach Road in 2008, but I doubt if it has!*

NEW BRIGHTON

In 1830, Liverpool merchant, James Atherton, purchased much of the land at Rock Point, which enjoyed views out to sea and across the Mersey and had a good beach. His aim was to develop it as a desirable residential and watering-place for the gentry, in a similar way to Brighton – hence 'New Brighton'. During the latter half of the 19th century, New Brighton developed as a very popular seaside resort, particularly for day trips across the Mersey from Liverpool. It competed with Blackpool and Southport for the valuable holiday week traffic, particularly from the Lancashire industrial towns, and many of the large houses were converted to inexpensive hotels. From the 1950s onwards, with the advent of package holidays abroad, the popularity of New Brighton as a seaside resort declined. After years of indecision, the future of the resort is being seriously tackled and opening of a fine new Floral Pavilion is an encouraging start.

The pier opened in 1867.

Work on New Brighton Tower started in 1896, two years after Blackpool Tower opened, and was completed in 1900. It was, at 567 feet, the tallest structure in Britain. It was dogged by misfortune from its early days. Six workmen were killed during construction and, shortly after opening, a young man jumped to his death. It was closed at the outbreak of War in 1914 and failure to maintain the structure thereafter led to a serious deterioration that led to its demolition by 1921. The ballroom, which had been built under the superstructure, was retained and was a popular venue for concerts and dances until it was destroyed by fire in 1969.

The opening of New Brighton Bath in 1934. The largest swimming bath in the world at the time of opening, it could hold over 4,000 bathers and 20,000 spectators. A favourite venue for beauty contests and concerts, it fell into disrepair and, after storms which damaged its structure, it was demolished in 1990.

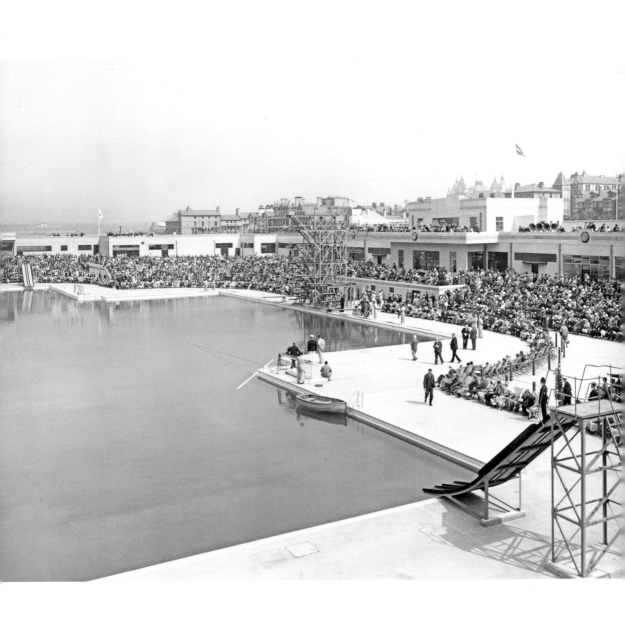

FINAL DAYS OF THE CENTRAL AND SOUTH DOCKS

The introduction of containers signalled the end of the working life of the Central and South Docks. Mersey Dock and Harbour Board realised it had to consolidate its operation and decided to concentrate activity in the North Docks, condemning the rest of the network to decades of decay and neglect. These photographs, taken by Pat Weekes, capture the end of an era for docks which once handled cargoes from all over the world.

Coburg Dock, dominated by the huge granaries which survived until 1986.

Photograph Pat Weekes

A rusting cargo ship berthed in Queens Dock.

Tugs moored alonside Waterloo Dock.

SEFTON PARK

In *Liverpool City of Architecture*, Professor Quentin Hughes wrote: 'Few cities in the world can compare with the green swathes of South Liverpool where parks have been laid out almost linking each other and where splendid tree-lined avenues radiate from the city centre ... South Liverpool must be one of the loveliest places in any European city.' Sefton Park is the jewel in the crown, some 400 acres of mature trees, lakes and waterways, open spaces and magnificent buildings and ornaments. Surrounded by impressive villas, it was an inspired decision of the Town Council to bring much needed green space into the sprawling metroplis. Now approaching its 150th anniversary, it has undergone substantial renovation in recent years which has cleared waterways, restored key buildings (and added new ones) and ensured its survival for future generations to enjoy.

The splendid iron bridge is a dramatic background to this family photograph, c1890.

The Palm House, built in 1896, has been lovingly restored.

The much-loved pirate ship, photographed in 1979, has sadly been removed.

LIVERPOOL'S LIBRARIES: A PRICELESS LEGACY

Liverpool has too many good buildings at risk. The news that Everton Library is on track to receive a major renovation is very welcome news. Libraries have had a very difficult time in recent years. Nationally, local authorities have been closing them down as spending cuts squeeze their budgets, citing declining use and the need to protect more essential services.

I am of a generation brought up to use and value libraries. For many, they have been a source of inspiration, a treasure trove of learning they could never afford themselves. Everton Library, in the heart of a deprived community, provided a priceless resource for adults and children alike. Designed by a very talented City Surveyor, Thomas Shelmerdine (who was also responsible for Kensington, Toxteth and Garston Libraries amongst other buildings) and opened in 1896, it is one of Liverpool's finest art nouveau buildings.

Liverpool has a proud place in the public library movement. It was a Liverpool-born (and Liverpool MP), William Ewart, who promoted the first Public Libraries Act in 1850, which led to the first public library opening in Duke Street (the building is still there although now used for commercial offices). In order to get the Bill through Parliament, William Ewart was forced to make an important compromise: only boroughs with populations of more than 10,000 would be allowed to open libraries. Sir William Brown MP realised the Duke Street building was inadequate and personally funded the entire cost of the Brown Library, which he opened in 1860 on Shaw's Brow (now William Brown Street). The new library attracted magnificent donations, including the famous art library of Hugh Frederick Hornby.

Liverpool did not rest on its laurels and its pioneering library work continued. Books were loaned to prisons in 1853 – anticipating the prison library service and this was followed by book loans to hospitals (1856), books to the blind (1857) and music being issued (1859). Branch libraries were opened in Everton (1853) and Toxteth (1853). The rate that boroughs could charge for libraries was increased to one penny in 1855 but it was not enough for councils to fund new libraries, and the growth of libraries was heavily dependent on the donations of philanthropists. In Liverpool's case, Andrew Carnegie, the Scottish-born steel magnate, personally funded six branch libraries – Sefton Park, Walton, West Derby, Garston, Kirkdale and Old Swan. Without his help, libraries in Liverpool would have made no progress until after 1919, when the penny rate was lifted.

Everton Library, St Domingo Road.

Toxteth Library, Windsor Street.

119

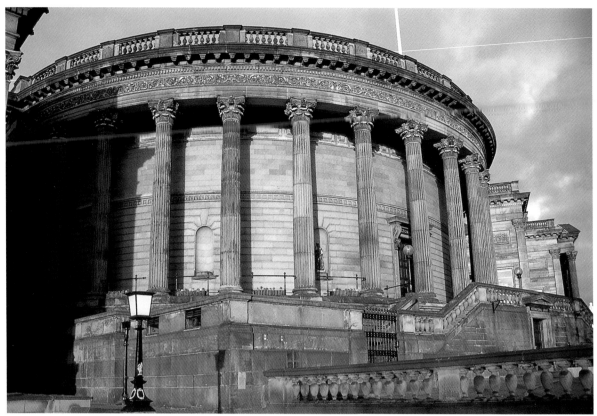

The drum-shaped Picton Reading Room, one of the magnificent civic buildings in William Brown Street.

The circular reading room. Modelled on the British Museum Reading Room, it is being renovated and due to reopen in 2013.

Kensington Library, again by
Shelmerdine, showing his
adept handling of decoration.

Garston Library, a lovely Arts and Crafts building by Shelmerdine.

RICHMOND FAIR

Richmond Fair was erected by Thomas and William Dobb in 1787 as a market for the sale of woollen goods. Like many other markets, it had galleries with rooms let out to other dealers. The market survived in the face of opposition from the Town Council, who zealously guarded their control over markets within their area of jurisdiction. The Fair continued but it slowly declined for, by 1873, Picton was writing: *'Leaving St Joseph's Church, and ascending Rose Place, we turn along Fox Street to the right. On the left side, about midway between Rose Place and Richmond Row, opposite the end of Great Richmond Street, we turn under a low-browed arch, along a short passage, and find ourselves in an irregular open area of about 1,200 square yards, surrounded by covered galleries open to the area in two storeys. The aspect is something like that of a dilapidated eastern caravanserai, or one of the Russian bazaars. Figures in caftans and heavy boots, smoking and drinking vodka; or the impassable Eastern, with coloured turban and yellow slippers, sitting cross-legged and indulging in the mild chibouk, would seem more suitable occupants than the groups of squalid children amusing themselves on the muddy earthen floor of the area, or roaming about the wooden galleries.'*

One by one, the traders left, and the Fair became cottages, occupied mainly by washerwomen. The photographs show the Fair shortly before its end. It was demolished in 1910.

RODNEY STREET

Rodney Street is one of the few nineteenth century streets that would still be familiar to its 1880s inhabitants. On the face of it, not a great deal has changed, except for the level of traffic. The road is named after Admiral Rodney, victor over the Comte de Grasse at the Battle of St Vincent in 1780. The battle, also named the Moonlight Battle because it took place at night, propelled Rodney into a public figurehead celebrated in the names of streets and pubs throughout England. At that time, the future Rodney Street was open fields but, by the turn of the century, there was a sprinkling of houses. Most of the building took place over the next 20 to 30 years.

Picton, writing in 1872, comments that: *The houses generally are of respectable size and character, many of them mansions of some pretension … It has had for some time a hard struggle to maintain its respectability, but there are signs of its following the usual course. After a reign longer or shorter of quiet dignity, the physicians and surgeons begin to colonise. The dentist follows; then a modest-looking display of wares in the parlour window indicates the modiste, or the brilliant red and blue jars give token of the druggist and apothecary. By-and-by a shop window is boldly put forth radiant with plate glass and gold, and so gradually a change comes over the spirit of the locality; the tradesman pushes out the gentleman and trade reigns supreme. Rodney Street is at present in the transition state, when there is a tripartite division between the private house, the doctor and the shopkeeper, but in the end the triumph of the trader is inevitable.*

Picton, as it turned out was over-pessimistic. Rodney Street is still that tripartite balance between private residencies, medical consultants and traders but it retains its elegance and has escaped relatively unscathed for its two hundred years of existence.

LIVERPOOL FROM THE AIR

One of the best ways of understanding how Liverpool has changed is through aerial photography. All the following photographs were taken in the early 1930s and show a very different city, when a population of over 850,000 was squeezed into a considerably smaller area than today's Liverpool.

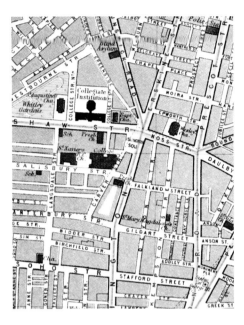

Islington and Shaw Street. The Gothic facade of the Collegiate Institute is surrounded by tightly packed terraced streets. Below it is another famous school, St Francis Xavier's College. Modern housing estates have replaced most of the terraced houses to the left of Islington.

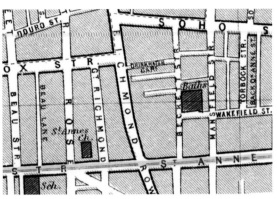

St Anne Street and Richmond Row.
The church, bottom left, is St Anne's
Church on St Anne Street. On the right
hand side of Richmond Row, open-air baths
on Birkett Street were one option for
hardier locals. The area has since been
cleared of most of its Victorian legacy and
now houses a mix of business units.

Lime Street Station and the City Centre.
The iron and glass vaulted roof of Lime
Street Station is the dominant feature at the
top of the photograph. To its right is the
white Portland stone exterior of the Adelphi
Hotel and, facing it, the original Lewis's
department store (destroyed by enemy
bombing in 1941). Below Lewis's is the roof
of Central Station, removed in the early
1970s. Other features include St John's
Market, a victim of 1960s redevelopment.
Below it is the Theatre Royal in Williamson
Square, another sad loss.

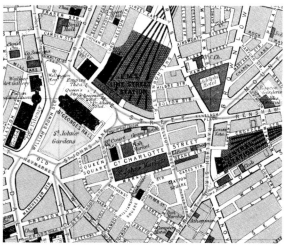

St George's Hall. The soot blackened exterior of St George's Hall, on the immediate left, illustrates the effects of a century of pollution. Across the road is the market area, with the long roof of St John's Market clearly visible. At the foot of St John's Gardens, work has commenced on the Mersey Tunnel, dating the photograph to the start of the 1930s.

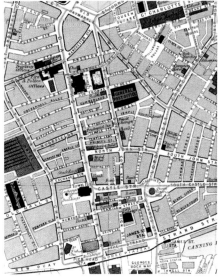

Central Liverpool from above Prince's Dock. St Nicholas's Church is a familiar landmark, bottom right, but significant changes have taken place elsewhere. The white-stoned Cotton Exchange (bottom left) can be seen in front of the long roof of Exchange Station. One of Liverpool's finest Edwardian Baroque buildings, its facade was replaced in the 1960s – another important architectural loss, The demolition of St Paul's church is taking place to its left (which dates the photograph to 1931). Built in the eighteenth century as a provincial version of Wren's St Paul's Cathedral, it had a fine interior although its acoustics were reputedly dreadful. It was replaced by Liverpool Stadium, a much-loved venue for boxing, wrestling and concerts (and in turn demolished in the 1980s). The tall warehouses lining New Quay, facing Prince's Dock, were removed to make way for the Mersey Tunnel exit and road widening.

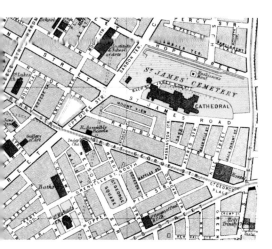

Liverpool Cathedral. The building of the Cathedral is progressing rapidly. The Lady Chapel is complete but work on the tower has just started. The housing fronting the Cathedral was removed in the 1970s and included the fine Jacobean-style David Lewis Hostel and Theatre (bottom right). Apart from a few old industrial buildings, all the buildings in the bottom half of the photograph have been demolished.

Harrington Dock. Liverpool Overhead
Railway winds its way along Sefton Street
before crossing Herculaneum Dock and
entering the tunnel to its terminus at
Dingle. The gasometer on Beaufort Street
is next to Beaufort Street Board School
(recently demolished). In front of it are
the chimneys and remains of the Mersey
Forge, reminders of a once-important
industry. Above the gasometer, a mill
without sails (High Park Mills) is another
relic of the area's milling history.

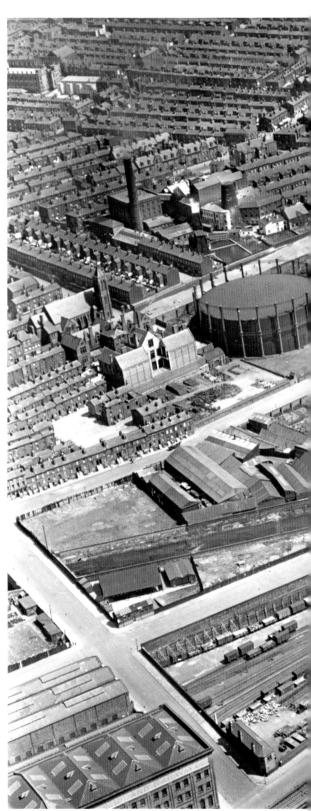

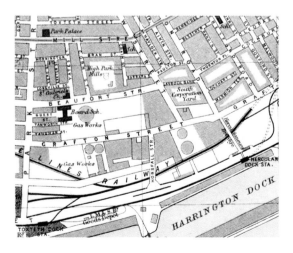

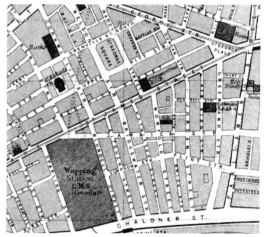

Park Lane and Jamaica Street. Another area which has since changed beyond recognition. The landmarks are the railway sheds of Wapping Station Goods Warehouse, which ran the length of Blundell Street and the magnificent classical St Michael's Church on Pitt Street – one of the city's most significant war losses. Much of the immediate area around Pitt Street was demolished in the 1930s to make way for tenements, with the loss of much fine Georgian architecture including Kent Square. The tenements in turn have been pulled down and the area is now largely a mix of modern housing and small business units.

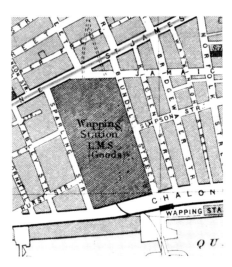

Wapping Warehouse. Wapping Warehouse runs across the foot of the photograph (although it has been slightly truncated today after enemy bombing destroyed four bays on the far right. The huge goods warehouse of the LMS Railway ran from Wapping to Park Lane. Fed by a tunnel from Crown Street, the station was an important link in the transport network. Only a few scattered warehouses remain of this once bustling area.

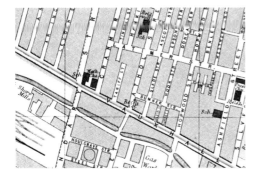

Vauxhall Road. The Leeds-
Liverpool Canal runs alongside
Vauxhall Road and through one of
the city's poorest and most densely
populated areas. At the time of the
photograph, Liverpool had a
population in excess of 850,000 (it is
now 466,000 but spread over a much
bigger geographical area). The lack
of any green space is a shocking
reminder of the lack of priority given
to making the city a habitable place
(although there is a basic concrete
playground just off Vauxhall Road.
The area has been tranformed since
the 1980s, in particular due to the
efforts of the Eldonian Co-operative,
and new housing and landscaping
along the canal have helped reverse
its fortunes.

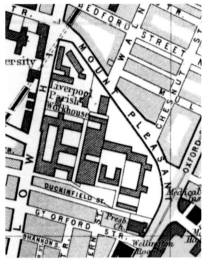

Liverpool Workhouse. A rare and fascinating photograph of Liverpool Workhouse. A town within a town, its high walls concealed the misery of thousands of Liverpool's poorest inhabitants. By 1910, over 5,000 occupants were crammed into overcrowded wards, where men were separated from women and families split up to preserve Victorian standards of morality. In 1930, the site was sold to the Catholic Church as the site for a new cathedral. The original plan was to build what would have been the second largest cathedral in the world (after St Peter's in Rome). War and rising costs intervened and the original plan was abandoned in favour of the modern Cathedral we know today.

Walton Vale. The Black Bull public house stands at the junction of Longmoor Lane and Warbreck Moor. The Cheshire Lines railway line running underneath Walton Vale has been decommissioned but, apart from the addition of further housing, the area is relatively unchanged eighty years on.

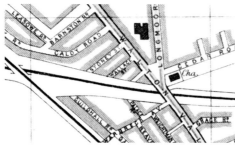

Calderstones. Compare this tranquil view of acres of green space with that of the Vauxhall Road photograph (p148). All Hallows Chuch is surrounded by playing fields and parkland. A cricket match is taking place in the field above it, part of Quarry Bank High School (top left). Although there has been further private housing added since 1931, when the photograph was taken, the area still retains its almost rural character.

Hornby Boulevard and Linacre Road. The shape of the area has been determined by the sweep of the railway embankment. The large factory in the centre of the photograph is the Bryant and May's match factory, destroyed in an air raid in 1941. Many of the terraced streets still survive.

Garston Dock. Garston Dock opened in 1846 and is still active, although nowhere near as busy as in the 1930s photograph. The significant change has been in the redevelopment of the area beyond. The gasometer and a solid core of the original terraced streets remain but, around them, new housing estates have been developed in the last few years. The area alongside the river is still reserved for commercial and industrial activity but looks rundown and in need of investment.